UNLEARN, LEAN IN, EMBRACE

N.D. Hill

Dedication

This is for my daughter, CiCi, to show her you can do whatever you put your mind to.

Acknowledgements

ii

Thanks to all my family and friends whom have always supported and loved me.

About the Author

iii

I was born and raised in Arkansas, and moved to Texas in my mid-twenties. I am a single mother who worked extremely hard to ensure her child was safe, educated, and have a 'I can do' attitude towards anything she set her mind to. My life revolved around my child for so long, I literally forgot to take care of myself. AND I am now exploring every possible way to love myself more and take care of myself. It's not selfish, it's self-care. Self-care is NOT optional, it's a requirement.

Introduction

S igns and/or nuggets of wisdom are all around you and they come from all kinds of sources. Not just from the preacher or a mentor BUT also from everything and everyone around you.

When you can't sleep all night and you're lying in bed and the TV is watching you while you keep your eyes closed and hoping that you can fall back asleep. The reason you woke up could have been you're a light sleeper and you heard a family member go to the bathroom down the hall, or you got too hot under the bed covers, or you had to get up to use the bathroom, or simply your brain turned on.

In all of these moments, there were things that could teach you something…. right? Wear ear plugs or have white noise playing in the background, wear less clothes to bed, stop drinking liquids at least 2 or 3 hours before bed, or maybe just learn to meditate. All good solves…. right. This book is not about logic. This book is about how to look at things in a different way to help YOU find your inner peace, find your inner JOY, or whatever calms you internally so that you are not using your energy on things that do NOT serve you.

First, let's unlearn a few things. Second, learn to LEAN IN. And Third, but no lastly Embrace. First, we will change the way you think & feel about what you thought you could NOT change (Unlearn). We will find ways that don't require such a fight and/or struggle which require a lot of energy and figure out ways to use little to none towards people that don't deserve it (Lean In). And thirdly, we will change our thinking so that we can perceive ourselves in a more positive manner; as well as, embrace all the things that make you amazing (Embrace).

UNLEARN

This is by the far the biggest hurdle. This involves you and your thoughts and your beliefs. It's a self- evaluation to some degree – right? How many times have you seen someone at the mall and thought – WOW did that person get dressed in the dark? Or that person is high maintenance? Or even, that person is arrogant. NONE of these initial thoughts are wrong per se. But you should instantly follow up any of those negative thoughts with a positive one. Force your brain to start being more positive. I know…. I know…. you hear it everywhere. Think more positive. Positive vibes.

If you are a faith-based person, you are told to SEEK AND YE SHALL FIND. Or DO UNTO OTHERS AS YOU WILL HAVE THEM DO UNTO YOU. Whatever you believe in the universe, GOD, Good Deeds, Karma, whatever your thing is…. that's what you should draw upon. They all have the same general message – right? It's the power of positivity and HOPE to gain/receive the BEST that's available to you. Whatever the BEST is in the moment or situation.

This is the start of something GREAT and so much bigger than you. To unlearn that the first initial thoughts about a situation are most likely negative. Why is it so easy to accept the negative so quickly and it's so difficult to LEARN how to be positive? The world may NEVER know why BUT you can LEARN to be more positive and believe that you deserve ALL the GOOD things that are available to you too.

As I get older my body does NOT handle the stressors of the world as it uses to. I grew up "knowing" I had to fight for everything I wanted out of life. I had to work twice as hard as the other person to get a well-paying job. I had to stay at jobs longer than I wanted to because I didn't get the luxury to quit because I was unhappy with being a single mother and in technology field. I have this demeanor of everything is fine when I knowingly could not pursue my own passions because I had to take care of my family and provide. I told myself I would be able to travel one day and not have to put myself so low on the priority list that I was not even allowing myself to have moment of self -care. Worrying about the next move, what I need to be prepared for, what I may need to be ready for so that I don't have to do even more work…the list of things just kept going and going. LIFE just kept hitting me at every turn. And one day I will find time for ME.

And then I started experiencing insomnia, even though I was really…. really tired. I worked a lot of hours because my job required it. But I told myself I would set boundaries and be present for my daughter too. So, I would work my 45 hours (occasionally 50 hours) and put a cap on the 50 hrs. I made sure I had my weekends off so that we could do something, but most weekends were me running errands I couldn't do during the week. And no REAL vacations for me. Throughout the year I made sure to take my personal days/vacation days and those went to sick days, doctor appointments, travel back home to AR to spend time with family & help them out. Literally GO…. GO…. GO! Even though I thought this was living. It was still time I did not truly spend LIVING. Don't get me wrong, I enjoyed spending time with family. I did have some down time per se. BUT I did not truly take care of ME. I just went with the flow until the year 2020.

I had been feeling off for a while and nothing seems to be getting better. I went to a Wellness Office, and they did labs and analyzed what my blood to determine if they could find what could be ailing me. I heard about this Wellness place from a co-worker who had started getting B-12 shots to boost her energy levels. The co- worker had mentioned that they offered other things as well to help with overall wellness. I figured I've been tried for years so it wouldn't hurt to figure out if this is my new normal or if they could help me gain more energy.

I bet your thinking why you didn't just do the normal things such as go to your normal PCP (primary care physician). I did but they were absolutely NO HELP. *They advised me to exercise more.* DUH…. I have a kid with extra school activities + I work out occasionally. Matter of fact, I had been in kick boxing classes for a while but had to stop because I was too exhausted to keep up with the workouts and it was not too friendly to my budget. *I was advised to eat healthier and lose some weight because of my BMI.* I wasn't eating terrible, but I can't eat only lettuce all day every day and drink water. BORING! *I was told I need to distress and get more rest.* I tried sleeping as much as I could, and that thing called LIFE just keep hitting me in the face at every single freaking turn. This was all normal.

The results of the labs revealed a few things. 1) That my body was in recovery mode from being sick, but I couldn't tell because I was already feeling tired. 2) I was anemic / low iron. I knew this because I had been on iron supplements for years. But this showed that my iron was really, really low. So, I was told to get liquid iron for better absorption. 3) That my body was not absorbing certain foods. So, I was advised to avoid certain things for a while. Which meant I could eat air and drink water.

I tried all these things and for months very little changed. I had a little bit more energy, but something was still off. I consult with my PCP again in 2021 and I'm a little irritated at this point because I'm still very tired. I had to advocate for myself because all I'm getting are sleep more, work out, and eat better….

clearly, they are NOT listening. I'm telling them these things are NOT working, so I ask what else can be done. My PCP said your iron is low so let's address that first. And asked if I wanted to explore a different option such as go see an Oncologist. This was a little scary because I was thinking how we go from Anemia to Cancer. The first Oncologist was a NIGHTMARE. She told me my iron reserve was depleted and that I need iron infusions to get it back to normal levels. So, I had about 4 rounds of IV treatments sitting in next to chemotherapy patients. It was eye opening and heart breaking. Then after my first set of labs after the iron infusions this doctor told me that I would need to wait another 6 weeks to determine if this treatment would work. At that 6-week check-in that doctor told me that she suspects I "could have something like LUPUS, HIV, or AIDs but won't be able to test for it until the next visit". That next appointment would be in another 6 months because we need to see how these 4 rounds of treatment worked.

WTH how do you suggest autoimmune diseases and then don't test for them. So, I requested a new doctor and they told me it's up to the currently assigned one to allow me to switch. I literally had to speak to this doctor and say I don't want you to treat me because I don't feel like you have my best interest in mind. Granted this doctor has dealt with a lot of terminal cancer patients so maybe they were desensitized. That's not my problem, I was not about to dwell the next 6 months to a year

NOT knowing what I have wrong with me. I need a doctor that's willing to get to the bottom of it. Thankfully I was able to switch a new doctor that I LOVE. She (Chandana Kakani, M.D.) is FREAKING AWESOME and listened to what I had to say. She diagnosed me with Thalassemia. Which is hereditary and it means my low iron is my normal. Taking too much iron is NOT good for me.

During this year, I also had a colonoscopy which resulted in a diagnosis of H Pylori. This is bad bacteria hiding in your digestive tract. If left untreated it could result in stomach cancer. About a week after the colonoscopy procedure, I began taking my first round of meds – I had returned to working my crazy work hours. As I'm working on a Friday, I notice I have a fever and told my manager, I may be logging off early. I've barely eaten and I'm unable to stop shaking. It's the end of summer and I'm freezing. I'm in long sleeve and sweatpants in bed under the covers and I can't stop shaking. My daughter is concerned and checking my fever every couple of hours and is concerned as my temperature reach 104. She forces me to go to Urgent Care. It's now Saturday. At Urgent care they take x-rays and vital signs. They were able to get my temperature down and I'm released within about 3 hours. They notice I have a rash on my arms, but don't link that to my symptoms. Then my temperature spike again early Sunday morning and my daughter drives me to a real hospital to go to the emergency room. This is during COVID and so the wait times are ridiculous. Thank God we were able to get a waiting room in the emergency department and I get a lot of tests. The test results are serious enough that I'm admitted on Monday because they diagnosed me with sepsis. Yes – sepsis which means I had blood poisoning. The rash is an allergic reaction to the H Pylori treatment. (I was also told that sepsis was most likely a result of an untreated UTI. If you've had a UTI (urinary tract infection) before then you know it's painful to pee – that was NOT my case. I still believe to this day that it the colonoscopy poked something that introduced bacteria to my blood, but I can't prove it.

This UNLEARNING lesson is that I had to learn to trust my gut. LOTS of lessons here…. a lot! I had to advocate for myself to find out what's really going on. Not to discount doctors by any means, but you must know your body and when something is off – you MUST dig deeper. If I had taken the first PCPs advise who knows where I would be now. UNLEARN that you don't know what's best for you. YOU do know what's best for you. Listen to that inner voice that's nagging you to look harder and explore more. And listen to the people that love you. Get extra help, pay for that extra test, don't take NO for an answer when you know there's more to explore. UNLEARN the norm that work is more important than taking care of yourself. Have a work/life balance – it's so important. And take opportunities to enjoy yourself as much as you can because you just don't know when your time is up. LIFE happens and try to enjoy it as much as you possibly can for as long as you can. And one more thing – LEARN about your health. Until I found my 2nd Oncologist – never even suspected that the low iron was more than anemia. My family didn't share medical information with each other. Maybe because they didn't want to burden the family or maybe because their doctor's didn't try to explore deeper. Regardless of the why, the lesson here also is that I have more information to share with my daughter that this could be something to know regarding her health history. LEARNING is part of the UNLEARNING process too. The more you know the smarter you can be when making decisions.

LEAN IN

Work has always been a challenge. As a woman of color, working in the technology field has been a challenge. Knowing that you worked harder, you have more experience, you have a higher education, and you will still make LESS than you counterpart. It sucks right!?!?!? And on top of that the expectation is to be in best of moods ALL the time. Regardless of the constant "stuff" flung your way. And feel free to substitute whatever word you see fit for "stuff". That was intentional. So needless to say, the word "challenging" doesn't do my situation any justice. But in recent months, I've noticed something I never noticed before. Actually, the signs started appearing or at least I started to take notice in the last year or so. People are put in your life at different seasons/stages. And sometimes it seems coincidental. But in actuality it's intentional. Depending on your beliefs it could be universe, God, Allah, Yahweh, Buddha, whatever you believe…. there's a great force that we can't easily explain placing people in your path. Sometimes we take notice and many times we don't. BUT I urge you to start paying attention to the people and/or conversations. And more importantly connect the dots of the people and the situations. What do I mean???? I'm glad you asked.

You know I have a few examples…. LOL. We are besties now. I've literally just told you about my medical history. We are FRIENDS until the end…. maybe it's just until the end of this book; but friends, nonetheless.

So, the month of October, I had been at my job for over 3 years. I've been promised to be promoted and have been "challenged" by my new boss to assume more roles. Yeah – there's that word AGAIN. It just keeps popping up. Keep in mind I had just been promoted 6months prior. And that promotion was just a title change because I had been doing the Managerial role for 2 years already. It was OVERDUE. So, I was just squared up for my work so to speak. And now another opportunity has presented itself.

Background: In April/May a co-worker with the same managerial title AND our boss also left the company for better job opportunities elsewhere. This left a big GAP with running the team now all rolling under me. It was about 8-10 people at the time. I now rolled under my old boss's boss. So, we had a conversation where he challenged me to assume more responsibility for the team in exchange for Director Title. I told him my expectation is for compensation for my "new responsibilities".

Fast forward to October and the Director role has not been filled by an outside source. I was also told when we revisited the promotion that I am out of cycle. End of story…. NOT. I've worked my butt off and set boundaries and kept this team going strong. So, to say I'm both tired and felt betrayed was an understatement. I reached out to 2 mentors during all of this. They are 2 strong women also of color that have been AMAZING along my journey. They have poured into me so much this year. And initially I had viewed my mentors as just doing their jobs. BUT in the past 6 months they have actually been teaching me to LEAN INTO them, my support groups, and into myself.

It's like when you are on a plane and the stewardess/flight attendants state that you must put your own oxygen mask on yourself BEFORE you can help other people. THIS IS SO FREAKING TRUE!!! (Read that again…. I will wait)

Think of it as pouring into yourself. Take care of yourself. Take time for yourself. Do things that make YOU happy and/or bring you JOY. If you like massages – schedule those once or multiple times a month. Get your hair did…. yes, I said "GET YOUR HAIR DID". Get your nails done. Treat yourself to a purse. Take a trip. Do whatever it is that you need and/or want to do for yourself. This as single parents or caregivers or whatever you do that makes you GIVE ABOVE AND BEYOND for others. You have to do the same for yourself. It's so important to NOT have yourself last on your own TO-DO List!!!

Why is this 1 thing so HARD?!?!?!?! I don't know but it's essential to your own happiness and self -care. Take care of yourself so that you can take care of others! Very simple concept, but just as hard to execute it. BUT I promise you it's worth it. I know this means you will have to say 'NO' to other things and/or people. But saying NO is FREEING! It lifts weights that you would otherwise NOT carry. It makes you a better person to dictate where you will spend you spare time because I promise you by saying NO it will free up time for yourself. Maybe you ease into it by sleeping a little longer, maybe it looks like hiring a babysitter so that you can go out with your partner or hang out with friends. Maybe it just looks like you take a day to do absolutely nothing – no errands, no chores, etc. No distractions from something that you really want to do. Whatever it looks like, carve out that time and/or space for you to do it. And if that means saying NO to allow it – I'm giving you permission TODAY to do it! LEAN INTO Yourself.

These women also helped me to recognize that just because I grew up with the notion that I should be silent and just do my job and wait for someone to recognize my talent is not necessarily the best path for me. Working at a job that does not ignite my passion or nurture my strengths doesn't work for me. I don't have to stay where I'm not being fulfilled in some way. I definitely don't have to stay at a job where I don't feel valued. I've always known I've had options and better opportunities elsewhere. BUT I really wanted to fix the issues because I knew that this job could be more fulfilling. HOWEVER, I also had to weigh the pros and cons. And the cons were adding up quickly. More work, less resources, executing order/plans from people that had NO concept of the amount of work it would take to complete, long ridiculous hours to accommodate the work, lose time doing things I want to do outside of work, not being able to spend quality time with family & friends, etc. The lists just kept going and going and going. So what am I truly giving up? My freedom to things I want to do because I'm shackled to a job that I am not passionate about. So, what are your options now? (I'm glad you asked…LOL)

My mentors did something that was just what I needed. Are you ready? They listened to me. They didn't just hear me and say girl this is what you do…. NOPE. They listened and then asked me probing questions like: So what are you next steps to explore what you really want to do? What are your passions and how can you utilize them in your current role? What does a job using your passion look like?

They also asked me questions like: what are you going to do for yourself this weekend? What does self-care look like for you?

They also gave me opportunities to do workshops/seminars for POC (people of color) that gave tangible and realistic advice on how to navigate corporate/technology field from a different perspective. From the lenses that I experience as a minority trying to get into the room. The line from the play Hamilton comes to mind "I want to be in the room when it happens!" There's a whole song about it…if you haven't heard it yet – find it and listen to it. If you have about 4 hours watch the play either steaming or LIVE. Either way, you will be thoroughly entertained and possibly awakened/motivated to do something different with your circumstances.

But back to me in my exploration of what to do – since I knew I had a decision to make. My only options were to STAY or GO.

If I STAY at this company, I knew I would encounter more of the same. More work, not enough pay, and continues pressure to work more than I'm comfortable with. My stress would most likely either stay high or increase. The possibility of reduction would be years away because of the stakeholders not fully recognizing that people are their most important asset. I would of course continue to be the advocate to change things; but at what cost? My health, my time away from doing things I love and/or want to do. (Is this worth it if no change actually comes for 2-3 years from now – and the answer to that is NO) And yes – I am thinking worst case because being completely positive at a pivotal point when I need to make decision could potentially delay my next opportunity and/or future blessings.

If I GO – I foresee a lot more opportunity. And frankly after the year I had in 2021 – I decided I would take as many opportunities as I can. Life is SHORT and I am determined to LIVE and ENJOY my life. I vowed to myself that I would enjoy myself as much as possible. Because I have not truly been living. I've been existing. I could go to another company with more of the same. OR I could go to another company and find the very thing I'm passionate about. Over the years, I've heard good nuggets of advice. (Of course, you know I'm about to share it…. DUH)

If you follow your passion, you will never work a day. Meaning it won't feel like work. Although I think when it's a labor of love it does feel quite different. Instead of forcing yourself to do it, it would come naturally or at the very minimal; it would come easier. Your passion should be something you enjoy doing and that could bring you joy. My passion is volunteering. By definition - volunteering is working for free, which is why I've grappled with how I would make money volunteering. And then I heard something very recently –

GREAT advice by the way. Maybe you should highlight this or write it down for future reference.

When you have an idea, go ahead and do it before you think of a million reason on why NOT to do it.

Find a partner to help you. There are a lot of people trying to do things on their own, and it's a little bit easier finding a person that can motivate you to keep going that is willing to help you. Everybody needs help. And if this partner is the opposite of you – that could work in your favor.

And finally, the most important part – when you work towards your passion DON'T think about the money or how to fund it. Just get started. The universe, God, Buddha, Karma will pave a way for you to get what's needed to keep you going. And many times, that money you earn will FAR exceed anything that you've ever envisioned.

The GO sounds way scarier knowing that I have bills and child(ren). But thinking outside of the box could also benefit me too. I don't have a big house; I can downsize to a studio apartment if needed. I don't have to live downtown or in the most expensive area. I don't need to have the nicest car – I just want one that is reliable until I obtain something I really want. Once I think about it – my NEEDS are minimal. It's the WANTS that have expanded my budget over the years.

And after all this brainstorming – for me to STAY seems like a terrible idea…. right? Correct. Making the decision to GO was the obvious choice. And it honestly didn't take my mentors or seminars to tell me that. I already knew it deep down, but they forced me to say it out loud. I had to LEAN into the idea of following a dream that I've had for so long. And the LEAN IN is the ACTION that's needed to move to the next step. I realized my fighting with EVERYTHING else had started a long time ago because I've been fighting with myself for so long. I eventually started projecting my fight externally. And that fight has drained my energy over time. To the point that it took a toll on my health. I encourage you to stop fighting with yourself and repurpose that energy to doing things that bring you joy and/or brings you peace. LEAN INTO yourself.

EMBRACE

Embrace all the good things that life still has to offer. Find those opportunities and go for it. Stop saying you will do things SOMEDAY. Make a plan and follow through with doing those things NOW. Do the things that bring you joy, happiness, laughter, enjoyment…. use whatever adjective you want. Do it now while you are in good health and have the physical ability to do things. Life goes by so fast. There are so many distractions now-a-days.

This year I was able to travel to Fort Lauderdale, FL to have a girls' trip with 3 other friends I've known since elementary school. Between the 4 of us, we've known each other for 30+ years. Crazy right…. You could say it's luck to have maintained friendships with women for this long. I say it's a blessing. We don't speak every day and there have been times where years have gone by without checking in. But the one thing that ALWAYS occurred was that we could pick up the phone or text and we pick up exactly where we left off. After husbands, multiple jobs, kids, etc. we still are there when we need each other. You are truly BLESSED if you have a friend or family member that is always there for you. Or has been there for you when you truly needed them. Embrace those moments! Embrace opportunities to meet up and hang out! Embrace the phone calls, text, social media messages, etc.

Example of things to EMBRACE and/or manifest:

- You are a Survivor
- You are Resilient
- You are Stronger than you give yourself credit for
- You are WORTHY of all that life has to offer
- You are AMAZING
- You are Beautiful INSIDE & OUT
- You are Lovable and you deserve to give love and to be loved
- You are Brave
- You are uniquely you and should embrace yourself
- You should LOVE yourself the way you love others
- You are in Good Health
- You are Blessed and Highly Favored with Increase on your mind
- You will have GOOD things coming your way
- You will be debt-free

You are _________________ (add your own words)

You are _________________ (add your own words)

You are _________________ (add your own words)

This book may be short, but when you think about it – who has time to read a 200-page novel these days. This should be short, sweet, sarcastic, and to the point. This is intentionally written like a conversation with a friend. I hope that this book conveyed that you are loved and deserve all the GREAT things that life has to offer. We do have a lot of pivotal moments where we need to make hard decisions. Some result in not-so-great moments, some result in learning opportunities. But my biggest hope for you – is that most decisions result with you being able to UNLEARN something that was holding you back, LEAN IN to propel you forward, and EMBRACE the opportunity to be the best you.

Thank you for taking time to read this. It was my absolute pleasure to share this with you. I sincerely hope my words brought you as many smiles as it did for me while writing it!